# Revival
## LEADER GUIDE

# Revival

Faith as Wesley Lived It

**Revival: Faith as Wesley Lived It**
978-1-426-77884-1          *Also available as an eBook*

**Revival: Faith as Wesley Lived It—Large Print Edition**
978-1-630-88294-5

**Revival: DVD**
978-1-426-77682-3

**Revival: Leader Guide**
978-1-426-77883-4          *Also available as an eBook*

**Revival: Youth Study Book**
978-1-426-78868-0          *Also available as an eBook*

**Revival: Children's Leader Guide**
978-1-426-78871-0

**For more information, visit www.AdamHamilton.org.**

---

## Also by Adam Hamilton

*24 Hours That Changed the World*

*Christianity and World Religions*

*Christianity's Family Tree*

*Confronting the Controversies*

*Enough*

*Final Words from the Cross*

*Forgiveness*

*Leading Beyond the Walls*

*Love to Stay*

*Making Sense of the Bible*

*Not a Silent Night*

*Seeing Gray in a World of Black and White*

*Selling Swimsuits in the Arctic*

*The Journey*

*The Way*

*Unleashing the Word*

*When Christians Get It Wrong*

*Why?*

# ADAM HAMILTON

Author of *The Way* and *The Journey*

# Revival

## FAITH AS WESLEY LIVED IT

## LEADER GUIDE

by Martha Bettis Gee

Abingdon Press / Nashville

REVIVAL: FAITH AS WESLEY LIVED IT
Leader Guide

This book is printed on elemental, chlorine-free paper.

ISBN 978-1-426-77883-4

All Scripture quotations, unless otherwise indicated, are taken from the New Revised Standard Version of the Bible, copyright 1989, Division of Christian Education of the National Council of the Churches of Christ in the United States of America. Used by permission. All rights reserved.

15 16 17 18 19 20 21 22 23—10 9 8 7 6 5 4 3

MANUFACTURED IN THE UNITED STATES OF AMERICA

# Contents

# To the Leader

Welcome! In this study, you have the opportunity to facilitate a group of learners as they seek to find revival in their hearts and lives. In every Christian's life, spiritual vitality wanes over time. Churches, denominations, and even revival movements eventually lose their spiritual vitality. Adam Hamilton believes the seeds of our revival, and the revival of Christianity today, are to be found in the life and ministry of John Wesley.

This six-session study is based on Hamilton's book *Revival: Faith as Wesley Lived It*. In each chapter of the book, Hamilton presents key events and places in the life of John Wesley and the movement he led and describes the convictions and essential practices of Wesley and the early Methodists. But the book is more than just a review of history. Hamilton believes that by reclaiming the faith, heart, and practices of John Wesley and the early Methodists, we can rediscover the best parts of our own hearts and churches and that in so doing we might help spark a revival of Christianity in our time.

Many groups using this study will likely be Methodists or members of Wesleyan denominations, but all Christians will find much in the study that applies to their experience of faith. The life and ministry of John Wesley, and the revival of faith they sparked, offer many insights for both individual Christians and churches of any denomination.

Scripture tells us where two or three are gathered together, we can be assured of the presence of the Holy Spirit, working in and through all those gathered. As you prepare to lead, pray for that presence and expect that you will experience it.

This six-session study makes use of the following components:

- Adam Hamilton's book *Revival: Faith as Wesley Lived It;*
- a DVD with video segments for the six book chapters (10-15 minutes each), in which Hamilton takes viewers to the places described, starting with Wesley's childhood home at Epworth and ending in the room where Wesley died at his home next to the City Road Chapel;
- this Leader Guide;
- Bibles (each participant should bring her or his own).

If you can, contact those who are interested in the study in advance of the first session and let them know what they will need to bring. Make arrangements for them to obtain copies of the book so that, if possible, they can read the Introduction and Chapter 1 prior to your first session.

## Session Format

Because no two groups are alike, this guide has been designed to give you flexibility and choice in tailoring the sessions for your group. The session format is listed below. You may choose any or all of the activities, adapting them as you wish to meet the schedule and needs of your particular group.

In many cases your session time will be too short to do all the activities. Select in advance which activities the group will do, for how long, and in what order. Be aware that in some sessions, the format has been adapted to fit the chapter content.

Pay special attention to the part of the session plan called Learning Together. Besides study and discussion of the video, Bible, and book, you'll see a section called "Reviving Our Faith." There, participants will be invited to apply their learnings during the week by following a variety of faith practices, with the goal of sparking a revival in their lives.

*Planning the Session*
> Session Goals
> Biblical Foundation
> Special Preparation

*Getting Started*
> Opening Activity
> Opening Prayer

*Learning Together*
> Video Study and Discussion
> Bible Study and Discussion

Book Study and Discussion
Reviving Our Faith

*Wrapping Up*
Closing Activity
Closing Prayer

## Preparing for the Session

- Pray for the leading of the Holy Spirit as you prepare for the study. Pray for discernment for yourself and for each member of the study group.
- Before each session, familiarize yourself with the content. Read the book chapter again and watch the video segment.
- Choose the session elements you will use during the group session, including the specific discussion questions you plan to cover. Be prepared, however, to adjust the session as group members interact and as questions arise. Prepare carefully, but allow space for the Holy Spirit to move in and through the material, the group members, and you as facilitator.
- Secure in advance a TV and DVD player or a computer with projection.
- Prepare the space so that it will enhance the learning process. Ideally, group members should be seated around a table or in a circle so that all can see each other. Moveable chairs are best, because the group will often be forming pairs or smaller groups for discussion.

- Bring a supply of Bibles for those who forget to bring their own. Having a variety of translations is helpful.
- For most sessions you will also need a dry-erase board and markers, a chalkboard and chalk, or an easel with paper and markers.

## Shaping the Learning Environment

- Begin and end on time.
- Create a climate of openness, encouraging group members to participate as they feel comfortable. Remember that some people will jump right in with answers and comments, while others will need time to process what is being discussed.
- If you notice that some group members don't enter the conversation, ask them if they have thoughts to share. Give everyone a chance to talk, but keep the conversation moving. Try to prevent a few individuals from doing all the talking.
- Communicate the importance of group discussions and group exercises.
- If no one answers at first during discussions, don't be afraid of pauses. Count silently to ten; then say something such as "Would anyone like to go first?" If no one responds, venture an answer yourself and ask for comments.
- Model openness as you share with the group. Group members will follow your example. If you limit your sharing to a surface level, others will follow suit.

- Encourage multiple answers or responses before moving on.
- Ask, "Why?" or "Why do you believe that?" or "Can you say more about that?" to help continue a discussion and give it greater depth.
- Affirm others' responses with comments such as "Great" or "Thanks" or "Good insight"—especially if this is the first time someone has spoken during the group session.
- Monitor your own contributions. If you find yourself doing most of the talking, back off so that you don't train the group to listen rather than speak up.
- Remember that you don't have all the answers. Your job is to keep the discussion going and encourage participation.

## Managing the Session

- Honor the time schedule. If a session is running longer than expected, get consensus from the group before continuing beyond the agreed-upon ending time.
- Involve group members in various aspects of the group session, such as playing the DVD, saying prayers, or reading the Scripture.
- Note that the session plans sometimes call for breaking into smaller groups. This gives everyone a chance to speak and participate fully. Mix up the teams; don't let the same people pair up on every activity.

- Because many activities call for personal sharing, confidentiality is essential. Group members should never pass along stories that have been shared in the group. Remind the group members at each session: confidentiality is crucial to the success of this study.

# 1.
# Precursors to Revival
## *Epworth*

# 1.

# Precursors to Revival

## Epworth

## Planning the Session

### Session Goals

As a result of conversations and activities connected with this session, group members should begin to:

- explore the need for revival, personally and for the church;
- examine the stresses and pressures on individuals and communities of faith that diminish spiritual vitality, and compare them to stresses and crises of the churches in Revelation;
- explore the life and faith of John Wesley by developing a spiritual timeline;
- encounter the example of Susanna Wesley as a model for shaping the faithful life;

- explore lessons learned by Wesley from his parents and grandparents about handling disagreements and perseverance;
- commit to one or more specific practices based on lessons learned by John Wesley to rekindle and revive one's faith.

## Biblical Foundation

To the angel of the church in Ephesus write: . . . "I know your works, your toil and your patient endurance. . . . But I have this against you, that you have abandoned the love you had at first. Remember then from what you have fallen; repent, and do the works you did at first." (Revelation 2:1a, 2a, 4-5a)

## Special Preparation

- On the board or a large sheet of paper, print the question "How full is your cup?" Obtain a glass or a clear plastic cup; fill it with water just before the session starts.
- On a different place on the board or a different sheet of paper, print the following words down the side: *Who, What, Where, When, Why.*
- Tape together several large sheets of paper horizontally, for use when the group creates a spiritual timeline for John Wesley.
- Print and post the suggested faith practices from Reviving Our Faith, below. (You only need to write each boldface practice, not the entire paragraph following it.)

- Get or make copies of the hymn "Come, Thou Fount of Every Blessing" from a hymnal or online. Several performances of the hymn can be found on YouTube, including a video by the folk rock group Mumford and Sons.
- Remember, there are more activities in this session than most groups will have time to complete. As leader, you'll want to go over the session in advance and select or adapt the activities you think will work best for your group in the time allotted.

# Getting Started

## Opening Activity

As participants arrive, welcome them to the study. If group members are not familiar with one another, make nametags available. Provide Bibles for those who did not bring one.

Gather together and invite group members to introduce themselves. Ask the group to say the first thing that pops into their minds when they hear the word *revival.* Invite volunteers to explain the word or phrase that occurred to them. Ask for a show of hands as to whether, for them, the word has positive or negative connotations. If anyone has memories of attending a revival, ask them to describe that experience. Did the revival include an altar call, and if so, did they respond? Did the revival result in long-term changes in their lives? On the board or a large sheet of paper, print the word *revival*, its Latin roots, and its meanings as described in the Introduction of Hamilton's book. Invite the group to respond to these meanings.

How are their initial impressions of the word different from these expanded meanings?

Ask the group to quickly skim the Introduction. Invite volunteers to state what they believe to be Adam Hamilton's purpose in writing the study. Emphasize that this is not just a study of Methodism or of John Wesley's life. Hamilton's hope is, rather, to spark a revival of Christianity and Christians of any faith community by reclaiming the faith, heart, and practices of Wesley and the early Methodists.

Adam Hamilton compares our spiritual lives to plants that flourish or wilt, depending on whether we water them. Another useful comparison is of a cup that is sometimes filled and sometimes depleted. Point out the question written on the board or a large sheet of paper: "How full is your cup?" Then show the glass or cup full of water. Invite participants to visualize this cup as their soul. Ask them to reflect on the posted question. Distribute index cards and pens. Have each person print his or her name on one side of the card and then write a word or phrase on the other side describing how full his or her cup feels at the moment. Collect the cards and set them aside until the final session of this study.

**Opening Prayer**

> *Holy God, we come seeking to feel spiritually refreshed and revived. As we explore how to renew our own spiritual vitality and that of the church, make us aware of your presence among us. In the name of Jesus Christ. Amen.*

# Learning Together

## Video Study and Discussion

Briefly introduce Adam Hamilton, the book author and video presenter. From his website www.adamhamilton.org, we learn that he is senior pastor of The United Methodist Church of the Resurrection in Leawood, Kansas, where he preaches to more than 8,000 per week. Adam writes and teaches on life's tough questions, the doubts with which we all wrestle, and the challenging issues we face today. He is known for exploring the implications of the gospel for daily life.

Session 1 introduces John Wesley and the Christian revival he led. We start in Epworth, England, where John was brought up and learned important lessons from his family.

Before viewing the video, ask participants to visualize places that have strong spiritual significance for them. Through each video segment, they will visit places John Wesley might have called holy ground. Invite participants to look for formative influences in Wesley's early years.

After showing the video, discuss the following:

- Why did Wesley describe himself as a "brand plucked from the burning"?
- Wesley literally preached on the grave of his father. Yet he found his spiritual grounding in another strong mentor. Who was it, and what did he learn from that person?

Hamilton asks viewers if they have had experiences similar to those that gave Wesley a strong sense of purpose. Encourage participants to reflect on that question during the coming weeks.

## Bible Study and Discussion

Adam Hamilton uses some selected verses from Revelation as the biblical foundation for his first chapter. Ask the group to skim the first two paragraphs of book Chapter 1 to get the context of the verses. Then invite volunteers to fill in answers about the Book of Revelation beside the words you've posted: *Who, What, Where, When, Why.*

Invite a volunteer to read aloud the selected verses from Revelation. Discuss the following:

- The Christians in Ephesus and the other churches of Asia Minor were experiencing a severe crisis because, as a religious minority, they were at the mercy of suspicious neighbors and state powers. What kinds of crises do we face as a church today? What crises and challenges do we face as a society?
- What day-to-day pressures are you facing? What effects do you think these pressures have on your faith?

Invite someone to read aloud Galatians 5:22-23, cited by Hamilton in relation to his own faith. Hamilton observes that in his own life as a pastor, there have been times when he experienced spiritual burnout and could sense a diminishing of the fruit of the Spirit in his own life. Discuss:

- What evidence is there in the life of our church that people may just be going through the motions of Christianity without truly expressing the fruit of the Spirit? If you believe this may be true, what factors do you think contribute to this diminished vitality?

## Book Study and Discussion

Ask participants to scan the book text under the heading "Responding to the Times," then name significant events of religious conflict in the two hundred years leading up to John Wesley's birth. List these on the board or a large sheet of paper.

Invite the group to consider events, movements, or circumstances in their memories that they think have served to produce conflict in the life of the church today. After allowing some time for individual reflection, ask them to name some of these things. Ask:

- Would you say that we are in a time of religious conflict or malaise? If so, do you identify it as a time that might be a seedbed for religious revival? Why or why not?

### Create a Spiritual Timeline

Explain that in this study the group will be creating a spiritual timeline of Wesley's life. It will include not only significant events but also the spiritual highs and lows related to those events. Distribute paper and pens and invite the group to scan Chapter 1 and jot down what they consider significant events in Wesley's early life. There are fewer of these to note in these early years, so participants may want to make note of events in Wesley's parents' lives as well. After allowing a few minutes for the group to work, invite them to call out events to add to the timeline, including dates, locations, and spiritual dimensions of the events. Post the horizontal sheets you taped together before class and begin to create the timeline.

*Lessons about the Faithful Life*

John Wesley's father Samuel served the church in Epworth for nearly forty years, and his preaching undoubtedly shaped his children, but Wesley's mother Susanna may have had the greatest impact on young John's faith. Ask participants to quickly read over the information about Susanna in the chapter. Then distribute writing paper and pens. Ask them to write an obituary for Susanna such as might have appeared in the Epworth newspaper following her death. After allowing some time for them to work, invite volunteers to read their obituaries. Then ask:

- What practices from Susanna Wesley's life may have influenced the faith life of her children?

*Lessons about Dealing with Disagreements*

Wesley may have learned a lot from his parents and grandparents about managing disagreements. Ask the group to read the information in the text under the heading "A Humble, Listening, Catholic Spirit." Discuss:

- What is meant by the statement that Wesley had a "catholic" spirit?
- Hamilton suggests that the twenty-first century is as polarized as eighteenth-century England. What does he suggest are ways to embrace a catholic spirit today in the midst of divisiveness? What roadblocks sometimes get in the way of the church doing so? What are your

own personal roadblocks or reservations? What are your hopes?

- Hamilton observes that we have forgotten how to listen, as individuals, as a church, and as a nation. What does he identify as key elements of personal and corporate revival in our time?

## *Lessons about Perseverance*

Point out some important and difficult circumstances faced by Wesley's family: the death of children, family debt resulting in Samuel Wesley's imprisonment, and the burning down of their home. Form three small groups or pairs and assign one of these difficulties to each. Ask the groups or pairs to discuss the following:

- What are the details of this difficult circumstance?
- How did Wesley's parents react to this obstacle in their lives?
- What did John Wesley learn from this experience and his parents' response?
- How do you respond when life hands you challenges? What resources do you draw on for help?

## Reviving Our Faith

In order for us to experience a faith revival, it is important to begin specific practices toward that end. Encourage the group to consider undertaking one of the faith practices listed below during the coming week. For some, this may be the first time they have engaged in a particular practice. For others, it will be an opportunity to deepen and expand a familiar faith practice.

Call attention to the posted practices and ask the group to read them over. Give the group some of the information below about each practice. Invite suggestions from the group for other faith practices related to what they have explored in this session. Encourage group members to make a commitment to engage in one practice in the coming week.

- **Pray daily for children.** Suggest that group members pray for their own children, grandchildren, nieces, or nephews, and also for children in the church or neighborhood. At the recent funeral of a beloved ninety-nine-year-old woman, her granddaughter told how the woman had prayed daily for all her many children, grandchildren, and great-grandchildren. Further, the woman reminded them often that she was doing so. Even children who felt alienated from the church felt the power of her prayers.
- **Listen to children.** Suggest that if participants are parents, they might set aside time on a weekly basis to listen to their children, asking them about their faith, fears, hopes, and dreams. If participants are not parents, they might send a weekly e-mail to children in their lives touching base and letting the children know they are thinking about and praying for them.
- **Listen to the voices of others.** Encourage the group to open themselves to a political, religious, or cultural perspective that differs markedly from their own. Ask them to listen carefully to what is being said by the person holding those views and then, with that perspective

firmly in mind, to test it against their own convictions. If a face-to face dialogue is not possible, ask group members to peruse an Internet news source they may not normally read with a perspective that differs from theirs. Suggest that they be guided in these interactions by the defining Christian characteristics of humility, grace, and love.

- **Reflect on difficult circumstances.** Suggest that participants reflect in daily times of devotion on difficult times in their own lives. How did they respond? Was their faith strengthened or diminished? If they are experiencing crises and stresses at present, suggest that they invite the Spirit to move in them as they persevere.
- **Other.** Ask the group to suggest other faith practices that come to mind after studying this chapter.

## Wrapping Up

### Closing Activity

Invite participants to reflect on their own families, both the family of origin and any group they now call family. How has their faith been shaped by these families? Form pairs, and ask participants to tell each other about one incident from their family life from which they learned an important faith lesson.

Sing or recite the words of "Come, Thou Fount of Every Blessing" or view a YouTube clip of the hymn together.

Encourage participants to read Chapter 2 before the next session.

## Closing Prayer

*O God, fount of every blessing, there are times when we are prone to wander from you and your love. We give thanks that your love is there sustaining us in times when our passion for you is diminished. Through this time together, revive our heart for your ministry. In the name of Jesus Christ. Amen.*

# 2.
# A Longing for Holiness
## *Oxford*

# 2.

# A Longing for Holiness
## Oxford

## Planning the Session

### Session Goals

As a result of conversations and activities connected with this session, group members should begin to:

- explore in 1 Peter 1:13-16 the dual facets of intellect and passion essential to a holy life;
- develop an understanding of what it means to live a holy life by continuing to explore John Wesley's life and faith;
- reflect on what it means to be an altogether Christian;
- create and examine metaphors for restoration;
- be introduced to and make a commitment to one or more faith practices for revival of the spiritual life.

## Biblical Foundation

> Therefore prepare your minds for action; discipline yourselves; set all your hope on the grace that Jesus Christ will bring you when he is revealed. Like obedient children, do not be conformed to the desires that you formerly had in ignorance. Instead, as he who called you is holy, be holy yourselves in all your conduct; for it is written, "You shall be holy, for I am holy." (1 Peter 1:13-16)

## Special Preparation

- On the board or a large sheet of paper, print the phrase *Holier than thou*.
- Augment John Wesley's spiritual timeline if needed by adding an additional sheet or sheets of paper. Make available writing paper and pens.
- Get drawing paper and colored markers for use in creating metaphors for restoration.
- Print and post the suggested practices from Reviving Our Faith.
- Get copies of the hymn "Revive Us Again" or arrange for access to video versions on YouTube.
- Remember, there are more activities in this session than most groups will have time to complete. As leader, you'll want to go over the session in advance and select or adapt the activities you think will work best for your group in the time allotted.

# Getting Started

**Opening Activity**

Welcome participants and introduce any who are new to the study. Remind the group of the faith practices they were encouraged to try last week, and ask volunteers for observations about their experiences. Any of the suggested practices might become long-term commitments. Remind the group that these require practice, as the name indicates, and that it takes time to habituate any activity.

Invite group members to respond to the phrase *Holier than thou*, shown on the board or on paper. When hearing that phrase, what do they think of? Are their impressions positive or negative when someone is described that way? What are some other words or phrases that might be used to describe such a person? Tell the group that in this session, they will explore what John Wesley meant by holiness and why he longed for it.

**Opening Prayer**

> *O Lord, we long to live a holy life worthy of our calling as Christ's own. Guide us this day as we seek to revive our lives, that we may more fully live to your glory. Amen.*

# Learning Together

**Video Study and Discussion**

Session 2 explores how Wesley's longing for and drive to achieve holiness proved to be formative in his young adult years. We visit Oxford, where John was educated at the prestigious Christ College and later served as a fellow at Lincoln College.

Before viewing the video, ask participants to recall their passions and interests as young adults. Invite them to look for the passions that pulled Wesley in his young adult years.

After showing the video, discuss the following:

- The small group John mentored attracted some derisive nicknames. What were they, and why was the group so labeled? Why the name "Methodist"? What are some defining characteristics of the Methodist movement?
- John's practice of foregoing haircuts was tied to the practices of the group. What was his purpose in going unshorn?

Invite participants to consider their spiritual lives. Is there a balance between disciplines designed to deepen faith and acts of compassion and mercy?

**Bible Study and Discussion**

Give the group some background for First Peter. Though this letter bears the apostle's name, most likely it was not written by Peter, who died around A.D. 64. Rather, it was probably written by one of Peter's disciples around A.D. 90. It was addressed to churches in the five Roman provinces that make up most of modern-day Turkey, and many scholars believe it was intended to be read in worship there.

Ask someone to read aloud the salutation of the letter in 1 Peter 1:1-2. Explain that the Christians in Asia Minor were facing a difficult social situation. Though they were not experiencing persecution *per se*, they were being marginalized for attempting to live faithfully, having given up practices of the idolatrous culture of which they had once been a part.

Following the salutation, have a volunteer read aloud 1 Peter 1:13-16. Invite the group to listen for what this passage has to say about being holy. Following the reading, discuss:

- How does holiness seem to be defined in this passage? Is holiness something a Christian achieves apart from God?

- If holiness is the quality of being separate from the ordinary, and God's people are holy because God has called them to live a distinctive life, how would you define living the holy life? What habits and activities do you think you would need to avoid? What habits and activities is God calling you to?

- The passage speaks of faith involving the intellect as well as the heart—both vital to reviving faith. The phrase "prepare your minds for action," when translated literally, means "gird up the loins of your mind"—get ready for thinking hard. What Christian practices do you think would especially enhance our ability to apply intellect to our faith? What practices might enable us to develop a passionate heart for God?

- Wesley scholar Henry Rack described John Wesley as a "reasonable enthusiast,"[1] a term capturing the emphasis on both intellectual rigor and spiritual passion. According to Chapter 2, what was the meaning of the word *enthusiast* in the eighteenth century? How is that meaning transformed in describing Wesley as Rack does?

## Book Study and Discussion

*Add to the Spiritual Timeline*

Distribute paper and pens and invite the group to scan Chapter 2, jotting down what they consider to be significant events in Wesley's life. After allowing a few minutes for the participants to work, invite them to call out events to add to the timeline, along with the dates and locations of those events. Add those events to the timeline.

Invite someone to read aloud the excerpt from the beginning of Chapter 2 that John Wesley wrote describing his spiritual life during the time he was in Charterhouse School as a child. Ask the group to reflect in silence on the following:

- How closely does this description of young Wesley's spiritual life match where I am at present spiritually?

Ask:

- What observation on Wesley's spiritual life would you add to the timeline to describe this time in his life?

Using different-colored markers, add these observations and comments above or below the timeline, depending on whether they represent times of spiritual growth or low points.

As an undergraduate at Christ Church, Oxford, Wesley was very much a normal college student. As he began work on a master's degree, his reading of Jeremy Taylor, Thomas à Kempis, William Law, and others convinced him that his faith was superficial. He longed to be what he called, in one of his most famous sermons, an "altogether Christian."[2]

To get a sense of Wesley's sermon, ask several volunteers to read aloud the sermon excerpt given in Chapter 2, under the book heading "Half a Christian?" Have them take turns reading Wesley's rhetorical questions in rapid fire and with passion as the rest of the group listens. Then discuss:

- Adam Hamilton observes that the weight of all these questions is meant to elicit a resounding "Yes!" What is your response?
- How does Hamilton define an altogether Christian?

Add any other comments or observations about Wesley's spiritual life to the timeline. Ask the group to scan the description of Wesley's small-group ministry at Oxford (under the heading "A Longing for Holiness"). Invite volunteers to describe how this small group pursued the holy life. Discuss:

- In the section "Half a Christian?" Hamilton describes the members of his own small group as "stretcher bearers." What does he mean? Would you describe the members of your small group in this way? Why or why not?

*Metaphors for Restoration*

Invite the group to read the Chapter 2 sidebar titled "We're All Junkers," if they have not already done so. Ask volunteers to summarize the author's comments about how restoring old cars provides a picture or metaphor for what God does in us. Distribute drawing paper and colored markers. Invite participants to think of a metaphor for restoration similar to the one about cars. It might be a derelict house, a piece of furniture, an abandoned city lot, an antique toy, or anything else that might be in need of restoration. Invite them to describe their metaphor using words or phrases, sketches or diagrams. Form pairs and invite participants to describe their restoration project to their partner. What is the lasting effect of restoration? Is it permanent? Why or why not?

**Reviving Our Faith**

Call the group's attention to the three posted faith practices. Give them the following information about the practices:

- **For the glory of God.** Remind the group that one strong influence on Wesley was Jeremy Taylor's book *The Rule and Exercises of Holy Living*. One theme of the book is that every action becomes religious, and every meal is an act of worship. Suggest that in the coming week, adults might stop several times a day to consider how the events of their daily lives can glorify God.
- **"For thine is the kingdom and the power and the glory."** Ask a volunteer to recite the doxology that ends the Lord's Prayer and lead the group in discussing its meaning. Invite group members to end each day in the coming week by praying the Lord's Prayer aloud. As they get to the words of the doxology, suggest that they consider each event of the day, along with their responses. For each event, suggest that they say, "For thine is the kingdom and the power and the glory . . . ," and think about whether their actions were to the glory of God.

- **Offer a breath prayer.** Jeremy Taylor suggests that Christians start each day and each action with prayer. One good way is to use a breath prayer. Psalm 115:1 includes two phrases that might be used. Encourage participants to repeat the phrase silently "Not to us, O LORD, not to us" as they inhale, and the phrase "but to your name give glory" as they exhale. This breath prayer can be repeated several times during the day. If group members like, they can choose another favorite verse or phrase from a Scripture or hymn instead and create their own breath prayer.
- **Other.** Ask the group to suggest other faith practices that come to mind after studying this chapter.

## Wrapping Up

### Closing Activity

Invite group members to look again at their renderings of metaphors for restoration. Ask them to reflect in silence on where they are in their own spiritual lives. Do they feel they're at a beginning point and in need of a complete restoration, like a car that needs a total overhaul? Are they in need of a "touch up"—perhaps having some rust spots sanded and receiving a new paint job? Ask one or two volunteers to share thoughts about where they are in the restoration process, as individuals and as a faith community.

Encourage participants to try one of the suggested faith practices during the coming week. Also ask that they read Chapter 3 before the next session.

Sing or recite together the hymn "Revive Us Again," using a hymnal or YouTube clip.

## Closing Prayer

*Gracious God, by your Spirit stir us to a new revival of holy living as altogether Christians. Guide us to new insights as we seek to revive not just our lives as individual Christians but also our life together in community. It is not to us, O God, but to your name we give glory. Amen.*

# 3.

# A Crisis of Faith

*Georgia and Aldersgate*

# 3.

# A Crisis of Faith
## Georgia and Aldersgate

## Planning the Session

### Session Goals

As a result of conversations and activities connected with this session, group members should begin to:

- explore justification by faith in selected verses of Paul's epistle to the Romans;
- develop a deeper understanding of experiencing God's grace and acceptance by continuing to explore John Wesley's life and faith;
- re-create and examine a metaphor for holding on to the bitterness and anger that often result from life's setbacks and failures;
- consider how faith can move from the intellect to the heart;
- make a commitment to one or more spiritual practices for revival of spiritual life.

## Biblical Foundation

> For what does the scripture say? "Abraham believed God, and it was reckoned to him as righteousness." Now to one who works, wages are not reckoned as a gift but as something due. But to one who without works trusts him who justifies the ungodly, such faith is reckoned as righteousness. . . . Therefore, since we are justified by faith, we have peace with God through our Lord Jesus Christ, through whom we have obtained access to this grace in which we stand. (Romans 4:3-5; 5:1-2a)

## Special Preparation

- Add more sheets to John Wesley's spiritual timeline if needed. Make available writing paper and pens.
- Bring a backpack and stones to class. Alternatively, a couple of tote bags can be loaded.
- Print and post the following suggested faith practices for use in Reviving Our Faith: "Learning from setbacks and failures" and "Spiritual reading of Scripture."
- Get copies of the hymn "Amazing Grace." A contemporary video version by Chris Tomlin can be found on YouTube.
- Remember, there are more activities in this session than most groups will have time to complete. As leader, you'll want to go over the session in advance and select or adapt the activities you think will work best for your group in the time allotted.

# Getting Started

**Opening Activity**

Welcome participants and introduce any visitors. Ask volunteers for any observations about their experience over the past week in trying breath prayers, glorifying God in daily activities, or using the Lord's Prayer doxology as a devotional tool. Did anyone choose to continue a practice from the previous week instead of trying a new one? Remind the group that such practices are tools to develop a deeper life in the faith. There are no rules about choosing and using a particular faith practice; participants should continue only those practices that seem to work for them.

Ask the group to respond with a show of hands to show agreement with each of the following:

- I have sometimes used the passing of the peace in worship to talk with someone about a church project.
- During the sermon I sometimes make a meeting agenda or task list for church activities.
- Secretly I wonder how the church would get along if I were not here.
- Sometimes it's easier to do a church job myself than to delegate. That way I can be sure it gets done right!

Encourage people who raised their hands to describe their experiences or similar ones regarding church activities and responsibilities. What is their motivation? Is it truly to live a holy life or is it about trying for salvation by doing good works?

Recall for the group that in the last session, they learned about John Wesley's focus on living the holy life. In today's session they will explore how people of faith, like Wesley was, are challenged when their desire to please God and be holy is not balanced with an adequate understanding and experience of grace.

## Opening Prayer

> *Gracious God, we give thanks for this time to revive our hearts and restore our passion for you. Open us to experience the depth and breadth of your love and your grace so abundantly extended to us. In the name of Jesus Christ, your gift to us. Amen.*

# Learning Together

## Video Study and Discussion

Session 3 examines Wesley's crisis of faith while serving as a missionary in Georgia and the defining moment he experienced at Aldersgate Street in London.

Before viewing the video, invite participants to look for John's description of what happened at Aldersgate. After showing the video, discuss the following:

- Though one might imagine that John Wesley would have had success in America, this was not the case. What happened, and what was the impact on John's faith?
- Wesley described his experience at Aldersgate as one in which he felt his heart "strangely warmed." What did he

mean? How did it change his understanding of holiness and its function in his life?

- What was the response to Wesley's preaching at Oxford and in churches around England? To what venues did he turn to preach?

Adam Hamilton speaks about the relationship between God's love and our response. Invite participants to reflect on what Hamilton has to say about it.

## Bible Study and Discussion

Give the group some background about the Book of Romans. This epistle, the longest in the New Testament, was among the last of Paul's letters. It probably was written around A.D. 56 from Corinth. Paul intended to visit the Roman church, which he had not founded or even previously seen.

As Paul wrote, he likely was thinking about the Corinthian church he was visiting, the Galatian churches with which he had been in dispute, and the Jerusalem church where he would be traveling with an offering. Of course, Paul also had the Roman church in mind, a church in need of instruction about the role of Jewish and Gentile Christians in God's plan. Of all Paul's letters, this one probably has the best summary of his theology: God has met the sin of humankind with the gracious gift of God in Christ, worked out in a plan for history inclusive of both Jews and Gentiles. This plan is the basis for life in Christ.

In the selected verses from chapters 4 and 5, Paul uses the Old Testament example of Abraham, a hero of the faith. Invite a volunteer to read aloud Romans 4:3-5 and 5:1-2a. Discuss:

- Paul seems to be saying that it's not just a matter of trying hard and God forgiving what you lack, but that God graciously justifies those people who are completely lacking in good works. How do you respond to that?
- What do you think is the relationship between justification and doing good works?

Form two smaller groups. Ask one group to read about Paul (Saul) in *Revival*, Chapter 3, paragraph 3, along with Acts 8:1-3; and ask the other group to read about Martin Luther in paragraph 4. Give each group a few minutes to choose someone to play the part of Paul or Martin Luther and plan a first-person report from the perspective of that character. Then have the two characters recount for the large group what actions they took to "justify" themselves.

In the large group, discuss John Wesley's efforts to pursue holiness and righteousness through his own actions. Ask group members to revisit the opening activity about church tasks and responsibilities. If there are those in the group who are deeply involved in church activities, perhaps to excess, invite them to reflect on their motivation for doing so and to respond to the following:

- There is a fine line in the Christian life between a passionate pursuit of holy living and an unhealthy legalism focused on rules and guilt. In your experience, how do you determine where that boundary should be drawn?

**Book Study and Discussion**

*Add to the Spiritual Timeline*

Add again to Wesley's spiritual timeline. Distribute paper and pens, and invite the group to scan book Chapter 3, jotting down what they consider significant events in Wesley's life. Add to the timeline the events identified by the group, along with the relevant locations. Then ask:

- What observations or comments on Wesley's spiritual life would you add to the timeline to describe the events that occurred during his time in America?

Using a different-colored marker, add these observations or comments above or below the timeline depending on whether they represent times of spiritual growth or low points.

*Explore the Storms of Life*

Ask someone to summarize the information in Chapter 3 about John Wesley's sea voyage to America. Note that in Scripture, storms often lead to great revivals of faith. Invite a volunteer to read aloud Romans 8:28, which can help us think about storms and their results. Discuss:

- If we place our failures in God's hands, they may become our greatest successes, and our painful experiences can become defining moments of grace, provided we learn from them. What experiences from your life can you cite that have functioned in this way?

- What is the role of repentance in these situations?
- Healing, grace, and new beginnings can take place when we let go of the right to be angry. In your opinion, is there ever a time when anger about a failure or difficult situation is justified? How do we determine when to hold on to our anger and when to let go of it? If we hold on, are there constructive ways to make use of it, or does it always pull us down?

In the chapter sidebar "Carrying Rocks," Hamilton speaks of a sermon metaphor he used to describe what happens when we carry bitterness, anger, and hurt around with us. Invite two volunteers to re-create and reenact that metaphor. Ask one to put on the backpack and another to gradually add rocks or other weights to it. At intervals, ask the person carrying the loaded backpack to walk around, then to try skipping, jumping, and hopping. Ask that person to describe the experience. Then have the person take off the backpack and describe how it felt to let go of the weight.

*Accepting God's Acceptance*

Ask someone to read aloud Wesley's own words about his experience at Aldersgate, in the book section called "Accepting God's Acceptance." Discuss:

- Up to this point, Wesley's faith had been built around rules and an obsessive quest for holiness that he could never truly attain. Wesley had an intellectual knowledge of the gospel but not a deep-down assurance in his heart.

Recall that in the last session, the group discussed a faith that included both intellect and passion. How would you describe the relationship between these elements?

- Since Wesley had been a Christian all his life, how could his Aldersgate experience be called a conversion? It may be that Wesley, for the first time, accepted his acceptance by God. What is meant by this?

## Reviving Our Faith

Call the group's attention to the two suggested faith practices you posted. Give them the following information about these two practices:

- **Learning from setbacks and failures.** Invite the group to reflect on the failures and setbacks they have experienced. Use Romans 8:28 to give these experiences up to God, trusting in God's grace to transform them.
- **Spiritual reading of Scripture.** Ask the group to try a "spiritual reading" of Isaiah 43:1-4a, a passage that speaks of God's acceptance and love. Spiritual reading consists of the following steps: Read the passage to yourself, looking for a word or phrase that jumps out or shimmers—something that says, "I am with you today." Say the word or phrase over and over, memorizing it and inviting it into dialogue with your inner self. Speak to God, giving to God what is in your heart. Finally, rest silently in God's embrace.
- **Other.** Invite the group to suggest other faith practices that seem to arise from this chapter.

# Wrapping Up

**Closing Activity**

Invite the group to share any observations or questions they have about what they have explored in Chapter 3. Encourage them to reflect on the difference between works righteousness—an obsessive and ultimately futile attempt to please God by doing good works—and responding with thanks to God's amazing grace by engaging in good works.

Tell participants that the familiar hymn "Amazing Grace" was written in the midst of a terrifying storm by John Newton (who, like Paul and Wesley, experienced a transformational conversion). Sing or recite the lyrics of the hymn, or show a YouTube video. Remind group members to read Chapter 4 before the next session.

**Closing Prayer**

Use the prayer Adam Hamilton reports praying with his friend Helen:

> *Lord, I believe that you love me. I love you too. I offer all that I am and all that I have to you. Help me to trust, like a little child, that you are always by my side. And help me to live for you and honor you in all that I do. Amen.*

# 4.
# The Necessity of Grace
*Bristol*

# 4.

# The Necessity of Grace
## Bristol

## Planning the Session

### Session Goals

As a result of conversations and activities connected with this session, group members should begin to:

- explore grace as a gift as presented in Ephesians 2;
- examine grace as God's active influence on us and as a quality of God's character;
- become familiar with the three forms of grace as articulated by John Wesley;
- accept God's gift of grace by continuing to explore John Wesley's life and faith;
- make a commitment to engage in one or more means of grace as a way of growing in the Christian life.

## Biblical Foundation

> For by grace you have been saved through faith,
> and this is not your own doing; it is the gift of
> God—not the result of works, so that no one may
> boast. For we are what he has made us, created in
> Christ Jesus for good works, which God prepared
> beforehand to be our way of life.
> (Ephesians 2:8-10)

## Special Preparation

- Print today's Scripture from Ephesians on paper or a card and place it inside a gift box. Wrap the box as a present.
- Add more sheets to John Wesley's spiritual timeline if needed. Make available writing paper and pens.
- Adam Hamilton discusses predestination in this chapter. Though it's important to consider this theological concept and how Wesley viewed it, it would be easy for the group to get sidetracked by an extended discussion. If you choose to examine this concept (under Book Study and Discussion), encourage the group to give it some attention but not to dwell so much on it that the gift of grace is overlooked.
- Print and post the means of grace that are discussed in this chapter, both those named by John Wesley and those pointed out by others.

- Again in this session, consider closing the session by singing or reciting the hymn "Amazing Grace." Get copies of the hymn or consider using a YouTube video such as the contemporary version by Chris Tomlin.
- Remember, there are more activities in this session than most groups will have time to complete. As leader, you'll want to go over the session in advance and select or adapt the activities you think will work best for your group in the time allotted.

# Getting Started

### Opening Activity

Welcome the participants and introduce any visitors. Remind the group that they are halfway through the study. If they have not yet been able to read the first four chapters, encourage them to do so. Ask volunteers for any observations about the faith practices they tried during this past week (reflecting on setbacks or failures; using spiritual reading of Scripture). Remind the group that these practices are tools to develop a deeper life in the Christian faith. There are no rules about choosing and using a particular spiritual practice. Although it can be helpful to try new spiritual practices, participants can decide to continue the practices that seem to work for them.

Display the gift package you prepared before the session. Invite the group to guess what might be inside. Then ask someone to unwrap the gift, take out the card, and read what is printed on it (Ephesians 2:8-10).

Afterward, ask for a volunteer to read aloud Adam Hamilton's story about the white chocolate cheesecake he received as a gift. (The story can be found at the end of Chapter 4 under the heading "The Invitation: Open the Gift and Answer the Call.") In this session the group will engage in a deeper exploration of the gift of grace and how we are called to respond to it.

## Opening Prayer

> *By your Spirit, O God, guide us as we explore more fully the gift of grace that is so freely extended to us. Open our hearts and minds to receive that gift and respond to your call. Amen.*

# Learning Together

### Video Study and Discussion

Session 4 will involve a deeper exploration of the gift of grace and our grateful response to it. We return to Bristol, where John Wesley began preaching outside to large crowds. It was in Bristol that the first Methodist preaching house was established.

Before showing the video, invite participants to look for the movement's organization. After viewing, discuss the following:

- Wesley knew that merely stirring the crowds with his preaching fervor was not enough. How did he move those who responded to his preaching into a deeper commitment? How did he organize the movement in such a way to encourage this?

- Describe the preaching house in Bristol. How did the building and running of the preaching house support the organization of the movement?

From its inception, this has been a singing movement. Adam Hamilton reads the words of the hymn, "O For a Thousand Tongues to Sing." Invite participants to reflect on those words as a reminder that our actions are a grateful response to the gift of grace.

## Bible Study and Discussion

Tell the group that, although this epistle is titled a "Letter to the Ephesians," it was apparently not actually written to the Christians in Ephesus and instead seems addressed to Christians with whom Paul was not familiar. It may therefore be a letter intended to be circulated to the churches in Asia Minor.

Today's Scripture provides a clear, brief summary of Paul's theology. Invite a volunteer to read aloud Ephesians 2:8-10. Note that this passage, unlike last week's passage from Romans, does not contrast grace and works; rather, it emphasizes that grace is a gift freely given by God to God's children, who have done nothing to deserve it.

Invite the group to scan the information in Chapter 4 under the heading "What Is Grace?" Discuss:

- The Greek word translated "grace" is *charis*. Like its English equivalent, charis can have many meanings: someone is said to move with grace, to act gracefully, to have style and grace. How would you define grace?

- Paul uses the word *charis* in two ways. What are they?
- How do you picture God? What qualities of character do you associate with that picture or image? Do you see God as an angry, vengeful judge or as Jesus pictured God in the New Testament or in some other way?
- Both the Greek and Hebrew words translated as "sin" have the sense of straying from a path or missing the mark. Hamilton uses the metaphor of a car out of alignment. What metaphors or examples can you cite for the concept of sin?

Form smaller groups of three people each. Assign to each person in the group one of the three forms of grace about which Wesley spoke (prevenient, justifying, sanctifying). Have group members open their books to Chapter 4 and scan the information about their assigned form of grace (found under the heading "Prevenient, Justifying, and Sanctifying Grace") and then briefly explain that form to the other two group members. Afterward, in the large group, invite observations, comments, and questions that arose in the smaller groups.

**Book Study and Discussion**

*Add to the Spiritual Timeline*

Again add to Wesley's spiritual timeline. Distribute paper and pens and invite the group to scan Chapter 4, jotting down significant events in Wesley's life as they have done in previous sessions. Add to the timeline any events identified, along with the relevant locations. Ask:

- What observations or comments on Wesley's spiritual life would you add to the timeline to describe the events associated with his preaching across England?
- What was the result of Wesley's experience in being rejected when he preached in churches?

Using a different-colored marker, add these observations and comments above or below the timeline, depending on whether participants believe they represent times of spiritual growth or low points. Discuss:

- What might we learn from the way Wesley organized his class meetings and how they functioned? Is organization essential to revitalization? Why or why not?

Wesley's faith and preaching were undergirded by Bible passages about God's desire for everyone to be saved and the offer of salvation to all people. Invite the group to scan the information under the Chapter 4 heading "Free Grace for All." Ask volunteers to describe Calvin's affirmation of double predestination, and how Arminius's (and Wesley's) positions challenged that view. Discuss:

- What is your response to these theological positions? What is Adam Hamilton's view? What do these views have to do with grace?

**Reviving Our Faith**

Refer the group to the Chapter 4 heading "The Means of Grace." Ask volunteers to name the practices Wesley mentioned in his sermon "The Means of Grace." Ask:

- How does Wesley define the means of grace? What does Hamilton add to the list?

Note that the faith practices used by the group for the past few weeks have included prayer and reflection exercises that would be characterized as means of grace. The sanctifying work of the Spirit is a process, and we should be able to discern growth in others and sometimes in ourselves. Discuss:

- Hamilton relates one instance when he experienced the sanctifying work of the Spirit in an instant. If this has ever happened to you, can you describe what happened?
- For Hamilton, the feeling lasted only a day or two. If that was your experience, were there any lasting effects that you can now discern?

Call the group's attention to the means of grace you have posted in the room. Encourage group members to choose one of these means, or some other means that come to mind, on which to focus during the coming week. Invite the group to consider the means of grace Hamilton names in addition to those cited by Wesley.

Also remind the group that memorizing Scripture can be a powerful faith practice. Encourage participants to consider memorizing this week's passage.

# Wrapping Up

### Closing Activity

Revisit the opening activity in this session (unwrapping a gift that describes God's grace). Point out that at the end of

Chapter 4, Adam Hamilton says some people reading the book have the gifts to be a pastor and others are called to share with others what God has done in their lives. Some in the group have already answered God's call to share the gift of salvation. Encourage the group to reflect on how they are called to ministry and how they can move forward in sanctifying grace.

Remind participants to read Chapter 5 before the next session and to focus during the coming week on one or more means of grace.

Remind the group that at the end of the previous session they sang the hymn "Amazing Grace." Close this session by singing or reciting the same hymn or by watching a YouTube video of the hymn. Ask them to consider Adam Hamilton's assertion that one reason our churches are no longer growing is that we have lost the passion for those who don't yet know Christ. Encourage them to reflect on the words "I once was lost, but now am found," especially in relation to those not actively involved in a faith community. Does God care about these people? Would their lives be different if they knew God's love, accepted God's acceptance, and lived each day walking in God's grace and pursuing God's mission?

**Closing Prayer**

> *God of grace, we thank you for your costly gift of salvation in Christ, which is given to us, to the people we know, and to those we have yet to encounter. By the power of your Spirit, galvanize us to share the story of this amazing gift. In the name of Jesus Christ. Amen.*

# 5.
# Works of Mercy
## *The Foundry, London*

# 5.

# Works of Mercy
## The Foundry, London

## Planning the Session

### Session Goals

As a result of conversations and activities connected with this session, group members should begin to:

- explore, in passages from the letters of Ephesians and James, the relationship between faith and works and the difference between being saved by works and being created for good works;
- examine works of mercy and how they function as a means of grace, by continuing to explore John Wesley's life and faith as well as manifestations of mercy in the life of the church today;
- become familiar with Wesley's understanding of the power of a dialectical approach to the Christian faith;
- commit to reflecting on works of mercy as means of grace.

## Biblical Foundation

> What good is it, my brothers and sisters, if you say you have faith but do not have works? Can faith save you? If a brother or sister is naked and lacks daily food, and one of you says to them, "Go in peace; keep warm and eat your fill," and yet you do not supply their bodily needs, what is the good of that? So faith by itself, if it has no works, is dead. But someone will say, "You have faith and I have works." Show me your faith apart from your works, and I by my works will show you my faith. (James 2:14-18)

> By grace you have been saved through faith, and this is not your own doing; it is the gift of God— not the result of works, so that no one may boast. For we are what he has made us, created in Christ Jesus for good works, which God prepared beforehand to be our way of life. (Ephesians 2:8-10)

## Special Preparation

- Make two signs, one that reads "Serving Others" and one that reads "Personal Salvation." Post the signs on opposite sides of your learning space.
- Print and post the passage from Ephesians. Underline or highlight the phrase "For we are what he has made us, created in Christ Jesus for good works, which God prepared beforehand to be our way of life."

- Add an extra sheet to John Wesley's spiritual timeline if needed. Make available writing paper and pens.
- Part of John Wesley's legacy is the ministries in which American Protestants are engaged. Do some research on ways your congregation is involved in such ministries.
- Have copies of the text of the Lord's Prayer available in the wording your congregation uses most frequently or is most comfortable with.
- Remember, there are more activities in this session than most groups will have time to complete. As leader, you'll want to go over the session in advance and select or adapt the activities you think will work best for your group in the time allotted.

# Getting Started

### Opening Activity

Welcome the participants and introduce any visitors. Ask volunteers for observations about their experience this past week in practicing one of the means of grace. Point out that some of the most powerful means of grace are ordinary activities. Remind the group that Wesley names public worship as a means of grace. While this may seem obvious, regular attendance at worship where the community of faith gathers is a powerful channel of grace.

Invite the group to take part in a "forced choice" activity. Tell them they will be asked to choose between two statements. Even though they may want to hedge their bets and abstain from making a choice, encourage them to make the choice that they feel best describes who they are as Christians. First invite them to listen as you read the following two statements:

- **Serving Others**. I believe that to follow Christ, I must respond to God's love by working to serve the poor, the hungry, the elderly, the sick, and the marginalized. Further, I must work to change unjust systems.
- **Personal Salvation**. I believe in personal salvation and in caring for others in the community of faith. I should use every means—prayer, Bible study, and worship—in order to grow in a personal relationship with Jesus Christ and in my love for God.

Ask participants to go to the side of the room labeled with their choice. Invite volunteers to describe why they made the choice they did. Also elicit comments and observations about making a forced choice like this. What discomfort or ambivalence did group members feel about choosing? Why?

Tell participants that this exercise is based on what is called a false dichotomy. In this session, the group will explore how John Wesley sought to reconcile these two approaches in his own life and the lives of others.

## Opening Prayer

> *Your abundant mercy and ever-flowing grace are*
> *gifts that are new every morning and every evening,*
> *O God of love. Guide us to a deeper awareness of*
> *that mercy and grace as we seek a better response to*
> *the wounds of the world, in Jesus' name. Amen.*

# Learning Together

**Video Study and Discussion**

Session 5 explores John Wesley's understanding that both personal piety and works of mercy are essential to faith. We discover the meaning of sanctification.

At the Foundry in London, Wesley demonstrated his understanding that we are created for good works, but that work began in the small group he had mentored at Oxford. Today we visit the Castle Prison and other sites associated with Wesley's drive to do good works.

Before viewing the video, invite the group to look for ways in which John Wesley engaged in works of mercy during this phase of his ministry and to think about their own works of mercy and what motivates them.

After watching the video, ask the group to think about and discuss the following:

- William Morgan, one of the small group whom Wesley was mentoring at Oxford, initiated the work in the prisons. Discuss a time when your faith was nurtured by someone unexpected—a young person, a new Christian, or someone else.
- Based on what you learned in this session's video, what is "works righteousness"? How did John Wesley respond to the allegation that, in doing good, he had returned to works righteousness?

Adam Hamilton describes the scope of Wesley's works of mercy. Invite participants to reflect on how they are responding to God's grace in this way.

## Bible Study and Discussion

Martin Luther dismissed the Letter of James as an "epistle of straw" because Luther believed it derided Paul's doctrine of justification by faith and overemphasized works. John Wesley saw it differently, understanding James to be saying that God's salvation was not just *from* sin and death, but *to* righteousness and godliness and *for* works of compassion and mercy.

Give the group the following background on this letter ascribed to James. Of the five people with that name in the New Testament, only James the brother of Zebedee and James the brother of Jesus seem to have the prominence that would make their authorship likely, but the question is far from resolved. The Letter of James has been described as a moral discourse, an ethics handbook, a baptismal catechism, a synagogue manual, and a book of Christian wisdom. Today's passage from James focuses on the relationship between faith and works.

Invite someone to read James 2:14-18 aloud. Point out that James focuses here on Christian moral conduct, not on the works-faith debate. Call participants' attention to the Ephesians passage that you posted. Note that you have underlined or highlighted the last sentence of the passage. Hamilton has targeted this sentence as the focus of Chapter 5.

Ask participants to name what Hamilton calls the two sides of sanctification, as well as the additional command he also cites. (See Chapter 5, paragraph 3 and following.) Discuss:

- What are two senses in which we might think of Wesley's faith as it relates to good works?
- How does Hamilton define good works? How would you?

Invite the group to name the corporal and spiritual works of mercy named in the book (as enumerated in traditional Roman Catholic theology). Are there other works of mercy that the group would add?

- Wesley believed that actively pursuing acts of mercy was itself a means of grace. What are some ways in which this can happen?

Ask participants to describe occasions when they have experienced God's grace while serving others.

**Book Study and Discussion**

*Add to the Spiritual Timeline*

Again add to Wesley's spiritual timeline. Distribute paper and pens and invite the group to scan Chapter 5, jotting down significant events in Wesley's life as they have done in previous sessions. Add these events to the timeline, along with the relevant locations. Ask:

- Based on what Wesley believed about good works and sanctification, what would you expect to be the fruits of these activities in the life of John Wesley? What seems to have been the fruitful outcome for the church?

- What might you add to the timeline to show spiritual highs and lows resulting from Wesley's work with prisoners, the poor, the elderly, and children?

Using a different-colored marker, add these observations or comments to the timeline above or below the line.

Protestant churches in the United States have continued these good works. Discuss ways in which your congregation or denomination is involved.

## Two Sides of the Gospel

Invite the group to scan down the text under the heading "The Foundry in London: Two Sides of the Gospel" to the paragraphs where Hamilton addresses the liberal/conservative and intellectual/spiritual divides that Wesley sought to bridge. Ask volunteers briefly to describe those divides.

- Hamilton believes that to come down exclusively on either side of these divides is to represent only half the gospel. What approach do you believe to be nearest the heart of God?
- If you had to place your congregation on a continuum between the two sides represented by each of these approaches, where would it be? In your opinion, is one side or the other overrepresented in the life of your church?

## Reviving Our Faith

Invite a group member to read aloud the paragraph near the end of Chapter 5 beginning with the words "The Christian life. . . ." Ask the group to consider what in their day-to-day lives they consider to be good works and to think about how these good works reflect their identity as Christians who are being perfected in the faith.

- **Acts of service as means of grace.** During the coming week, as participants go about doing the good works they have identified, invite them to offer these works in prayer, asking not only that they may perform the tasks to the glory of God and the benefit of others, but also that through the tasks their hearts may be filled with grace.

# Wrapping Up

### Closing Activity

Invite the group to name wounded places in our world—issues and situations that represent a gap between the world as it is and the world God intends. List these wounded places on the board or a large sheet of paper. Invite the group to pray together the Lord's Prayer. After the words "Thy kingdom come, thy will be done," name the wounded places, one at a time, that were listed by the group. After each wounded place, have the group say, "Lord, what would you have us do?" and ask that they pray silently. After all the wounded places are lifted up to God, finish praying the Lord's Prayer all together.

Suggest that some participants may want to use the Lord's Prayer in this way as part of their devotional time during the coming week.

## Closing Prayer

*O Lord, your kingdom come, your will be done. We thank you for your grace so freely extended. As we grow in grace, make your will known to us. Stir us to act with compassion, love, and mercy, that we may become more fully what you intend us to be as we are perfected in love. In the name of Jesus Christ our Savior. Amen.*

# 6.
# Persevering to the End
## *City Road Chapel, London*

# 6.

# Persevering to the End

## *City Road Chapel, London*

### Planning the Session

**Session Goals**

As a result of conversations and activities connected with this session, group members should begin to:

- explore perseverance—doing what's right when faced with opposition and persecution—in Matthew's Gospel, Proverbs, and the life of John Wesley;
- become familiar with Wesley's teachings about how to use money, how to approach dying, and how these two issues relate to spiritual vitality;
- create personal spiritual timelines to discern the Spirit's movement in their lives;
- evaluate their spiritual vitality on completion of this study.

## Biblical Foundation

> Blessed are those who are persecuted for righ-
> teousness' sake, for theirs is the kingdom of heaven.
> Blessed are you when people revile you and
> persecute you and utter all kinds of evil against
> you falsely on my account. Rejoice and be glad, for
> your reward is great in heaven, for in the same way
> they persecuted the prophets who were before you.
> (Matthew 5:10-12)

> Speak out for those who cannot speak,
>     for the rights of all the destitute.
> Speak out, judge righteously,
>     defend the rights of the poor and needy.
> (Proverbs 31:8-9)

## Special Preparation

- Make plans to complete John Wesley's spiritual timeline, displaying the additions made in previous sessions and adding another sheet if needed. Make available writing paper and pens.
- In this session, participants will have an opportunity to create spiritual timelines for their own lives. Cut large sheets of paper into strips about six to nine inches wide and about eighteen inches long. Plan to provide pencils, colored markers, and crayons. Be sure to have extra paper and tape on hand.
- Get copies of the hymn "I'll Praise My Maker While I've Breath" from a hymnal or an online source.

- Locate and bring the index cards that participants filled out during the first session. Have a few blank cards on hand for anyone who was not present at that first session.
- Remember, there are more activities in this session than most groups will have time to complete. As leader, you'll want to go over the session in advance and select or adapt the activities you think will work best for your group in the time allotted.

# Getting Started

## Opening Activity

Welcome the participants to the sixth and final session of the study. Invite volunteers to tell about their experience during the past week in reflecting on acts of service as means of grace. Were the acts transformed in any way by viewing them as means of grace?

Ask the group to think about a time when they faced opposition. It might have been in the workplace, at church, or in another setting. They may have been trying to change an organization in ways that would make it more just or they may have stood up for something that was right when others did not agree.

Form pairs and invite participants to talk about these experiences:

- What happened as a result? Were they able to persevere despite opposition? Did they pay a price for their stand? What were their feelings about the experience?

Afterward, in the large group, ask volunteers to share observations from their pairs. Tell the group that in today's session, they will be exploring how John Wesley persevered in the face of opposition, eventually sparking a revival and leaving a lasting legacy.

**Opening Prayer**

> *Ever faithful God, we give thanks for chances to explore times of testing when being faithful is hard. When we are tempted to give up, make us aware of those who did not give up. When we are discouraged, remind us of faith heroes who persevered in the face of overwhelming odds. Guide us by your Spirit as we seek to revive our faith. In the name of Christ Jesus. Amen.*

# Learning Together

**Video Study and Discussion**

Session 6 looks back over Wesley's life and the opposition he experienced. In examining his understanding of money and slavery, we learn not only about perseverance, but about its relationship to spiritual vitality. We visit City Road Chapel, Wesley's final home, where he taught us the nature of dying well, and the cemetery where he is buried.

Before viewing the video, invite participants to look for what the mother church of Methodism tells us about the movement's vitality, as well as what John's house reveals about his faith.

After watching the video, ask the group to consider and discuss the following:

- Adam Hamilton tells us that the chapel was particularly well suited for two aspects of worship that are hallmarks of Methodism. What are they, and how were they expressed during the early days of Methodism?
- What can we learn from the rooms in Wesley's house? What about its floor plan was particularly suited to his daily devotional life?
- What do we learn from Wesley's last words? from the words on his tombstone?

Also encourage participants to refer to the photographs and descriptions at the end of book Chapter 6, especially City Road Chapel, John Wesley's house, and the cemetery where Susanna Wesley is buried.

**Bible Study and Discussion**

Ask someone in the group to read this week's first Scripture, from the Gospel of Matthew, and remind the group that it is part of the Sermon on the Mount. The sayings in that sermon seem simply to describe different kinds of "good" people, but in fact they are not about general human qualities. Instead, Jesus was pronouncing blessing on those who anticipate the fulfillment of God's kingdom, all the while acting in accord with that kingdom. For example, those who are persecuted endure precisely because they are part of the community of disciples. And those who act righteously are actively doing God's will, as disciples are called to do, as well as anticipating

God's justice and coming to the world when the kingdom is finally fulfilled.

Invite a volunteer to describe the stiff resistance John Wesley encountered when he preached a message that Christ calls us to a deeper level of commitment and a serious pursuit of the holy life. Ask the group to respond to this question posed by Hamilton in book Chapter 6:

- In what ways does the faith of the church in Wesley's day resemble the faith in our churches today?

Also discuss the following:

- How do you suppose church members in the United States would respond today if someone preached a sermon such as John Wesley's "Scriptural Christianity"?
- When Wesley was barred from preaching in the pulpits of England's churches, he preached outside, often at the market crosses of towns. If a preacher today wanted to reach lots of people, what might be a modern-day equivalent of the market cross? Where in our culture might one reach out to those who are not part of a faith community? From whom might we expect resistance or hostility if we used those venues?

Ask a group member to read this week's second Scripture, which is from Proverbs. This passage addresses the gap between the world as it is and the world that God intends. Then ask participants to read the material in book Chapter 6 under the heading "Speaking Out for Those Who Can't Speak for Themselves."

Later in John Wesley's life, after attaining recognition and acclamation, he was still challenging unjust systems. Invite someone to summarize what happened when Wesley preached against slavery in Bristol, one of the centers of the triangular slave trade. Invite the group to reflect on the questions posed at the end of this section:

- Are you speaking out for those who can't speak? Are you standing against injustice, for the rights of the poor and needy, for the dignity of those who have been pushed down or made to feel small? Or are you playing it safe?

Martin Luther King, Jr., endured not only hostility and opposition but also death threats; yet he persisted despite discouragement and fear. Invite the group to consider the United States today. While some would contend that we live in a post-racial society, others insist there are persistent signs that the power of racism is still strong. Discuss:

- What prophetic word do you think Christians today should be speaking about racism?
- What kinds of resistance might we encounter if we speak out? From whom might resistance come?

## Book Study and Discussion

*Wesley and Monetary Wealth*

As the Methodist movement grew larger, Wesley became concerned that the increasing prosperity of Methodists might cause some to fall away from the faith. Invite the group to name the three rules regarding wealth that Wesley offered in his sermon "The Use of Money." (See the book section "Wesley's Concern About Wealth.") Print each rule on a separate large sheet of paper. Form three smaller groups and assign one rule to each group. Ask them to discuss their assigned rule and print a brief summary on their sheet.

After allowing a few minutes for the small groups to work, place the sheets in three different parts of your space. Ask participants to go to each sheet, read the summary, and jot down any observations they have, as well as questions or caveats. In the large group, pose the following questions to be considered in silence:

- What does your bank statement say about your spiritual life?
- What does your generosity express about surrendering your life to God?

The City Road Chapel was completed in 1778. Though Wesley preached about the importance of missions and believed passionately in caring for the poor, he also believed that buildings were essential to the work of the church. Discuss:

- How do we balance the need for church buildings with the monetary support needed for works of mercy and justice? Does one take priority over the other? How do we decide?

*Holy Dying*

Call the attention of the group to what Chapter 6 says about Wesley's "holy dying." Invite someone to describe Elizabeth Ritchie's account of Wesley's death. Discuss the following:

- How would you describe dying well?
- Wesley embodied Christian hope at his death. Is there also a place for lament in the Christian experience of dying?
- What about untimely or tragic death? How do we as Christians celebrate it and mourn it?
- Regardless of your age, what plans or thoughts do you have for celebrating your own life at its end so that it bears witness to the Resurrection?

Remind the group that of all the passages and practices of life, death is one that all of us will experience. Encourage participants to continue reflecting on what Wesley's life and ministry teach us about a holy death.

Sing or recite together the Isaac Watts hymn that Wesley quoted before he died, "I'll Praise My Maker While I've Breath."

*Complete Wesley's Spiritual Timeline*

Distribute paper and pens. Invite the group to scan book Chapter 6 and jot down significant events in Wesley's life as they have done in previous sessions. Add those events to the timeline, along with the relevant locations. Ask:

- What observations or comments on Wesley's spiritual life would you add to the timeline to describe these events?

Add these observations or comments above or below the timeline as in previous sessions. Invite the group to look over the completed spiritual timeline and consider these questions:

- What events and influences had a positive effect on Wesley's spiritual life?
- What were some of the negative influences on Wesley's spiritual life? How did they shape Wesley as a Christian and as one who fully embraced God's plan to use him to spark a revival and a movement?

*Create Personal Spiritual Timelines*

Look again at the completed spiritual timeline of John Wesley's life. Of course, it's not possible to know how Wesley viewed the various events the group identified; however, it is possible for Christians today to look back on Wesley, allowing the Spirit to speak through him, and discern his witness and impact.

Invite participants to create similar spiritual timelines for their own lives up to this point. Distribute the paper strips, pencils, and colored markers or crayons. Encourage participants to begin by indicating their birth date at the far left of the strip, then adding the present date at the far right of the strip. In between, they will construct a line, marking significant life events. They can either make a straight horizontal line or move the line up and down to indicate spiritual highs and lows. They can describe these highs and lows above or below the line as the group has done with Wesley's timeline.

For some, the process of looking back at events will allow them to discern the Spirit's moving in their lives, even when they were not aware of it at the time. For others, the movement of the Spirit may not be so evident. Encourage the group to take the timelines home to work on some more and reflect on their life events

# Wrapping Up

## Closing Activity

Encourage participants to refer to their own timelines and reflect on whether, spiritually, they are presently in a time of vitality or diminished energy. Ask volunteers to read aloud John 13:35 and 1 Corinthians 13:4-8a. Ask participants to consider the following:

- How well am I reflecting the love for others epitomized in these passages of Scripture?
- Do I express that kind of love only for family, neighbors, and those in my faith community, or do I also extend it to enemies and those who oppose me?
- How well does my faith engage my heart, head, and hands?

Distribute to participants the index cards they filled out during Session 1 in answer to the question "How full is your cup?" Remind them that if a cup represents our soul and water represents our spiritual passion and vitality, there are times when we feel spiritually full, but conflict, adversity, and daily living can deplete that vitality. (If there are some people present who did not respond to the question in the first session, invite them to do so now, thinking back to their condition when they started this study.) Ask participants to reflect on how they were feeling about their spiritual vitality during that first session. Would they answer differently now?

Remind the group that they have been trying faith practices throughout the study. Encourage them to continue using any of the practices that seemed helpful or to explore other practices. Revisit any lingering questions from previous sessions, emphasizing that it is fine for questions to remain unanswered. Invite the group to share any final observations about the study.

## Closing Prayer

Chapter 6 closes with a prayer that John Wesley invited eighteenth-century Christians to pray. Ask the group to join you in saying that prayer now. It can also be found at the end of the book.

> *I am no longer my own, but thine.*
> *Put me to what thou wilt,*
> *rank me with whom thou wilt.*
> *Put me to doing, put me to suffering.*
> *Let me be employed for thee or laid aside for thee,*
> *exalted for thee or brought low for thee.*
> *Let me be full, let me be empty.*
> *Let me have all things, let me have nothing.*

*I freely and heartily yield all things*
    *to thy pleasure and disposal.*
*And now, O glorious and blessed God,*
    *Father, Son and Holy Spirit,*
    *thou art mine, and I am thine.*
*So be it.*
*And the covenant which I have made on earth,*
    *let it be ratified in heaven. Amen.*

# Notes

1. See Henry D. Rack, *Reasonable Enthusiast: John Wesley and the Rise of Methodism.* (London: Epworth Press, 1989).

2. See John Wesley, Sermon 2, "The Almost Christian. From *The Works of John Wesley*, vol. 1, ed. Albert C. Outler. (Nashville: Abingdon Press, 1984).